973

EDUCATION RESOURCE SERVICE

D0321620

2 1 DEC 2010

2 2 JUN 2011

2 6 MAR 2013 -2 DEC 2011

2 7 MAY 2013

1 8 FEB 2014

1 0 OCT 2014

1 2 OCT 2015

1 8 OCT 2016

2 7 SEP 2017

EDUCATION RESOURCE SERVICE

East Ayrshire
COUNCIL

LIBRARY, REGISTRATION & INFORMATION SERVICES
Please return/renew item by last date shown - thank you for using your library

SIGHTSEERS
ESSENTIAL TRAVEL GUIDES TO THE PAST

CALIFORNIA

GOLD RUSH

A GUIDE TO CALIFORNIA
IN THE 1850s

JULIE FERRIS

KINGFISHER

KINGFISHER
Kingfisher Publications Plc
New Penderel House,
283–288 High Holborn,
London WC1V 7HZ

Written and edited by   Julie Ferris
Senior Designer   Jane Tassie

Consultant   Christina Parker
Illustrations   Inklink Firenze
Kevin Maddison
Ray Grinaway

Editorial assistance   Katie Puckett
Research   Prue Grice
DTP Co-ordinator   Nicky Studdart
Production Controller   Kelly Johnson
Picture Research Manager   Jane Lambert
Proofreader   Sheila Clewley
Indexer   Sylvia Potter

First published by Kingfisher Publications Plc 1999
1 3 5 7 9 10 8 6 4 2

1TR/0399/WKT/UNV(UNV)/140MA

Copyright © Kingfisher Publications Plc 1999

All rights reserved. No part of this publication may be reproduced,
stored in a retrieval system or transmitted by any means,
electronic, mechanical, photocopying or otherwise, without
the prior permission of the publisher.

A CIP catalogue record for this book is available from
the British Library.

ISBN 0 7534 0373 0

Printed in
Hong Kong/China

Contents

Introducing California

California was a Mexican colony until 1846, when it was claimed by United States troops. In 1850 it became the 31st state.

U ntil the discovery of gold in 1848, California was little more than a collection of Franciscan missions, cattle ranches and thinly populated coastal towns. As news of the gold find spread, people from all over the world began flocking to the area, seeking their fortunes.

Because of the vast numbers of prospectors who travelled to California in 1849, gold seekers are often nicknamed "forty-niners". You may be able to pick up a souvenir cartoon of a miner in a magazine or newspaper.

The town that has seen the biggest transformation in the last few years is San Francisco. Before the gold rush it was little more than a village of about 800 people. It is now a cosmopolitan city with a diverse population including Germans, French, Australians, Chinese, Irish, Mexicans and Americans.

San Francisco has a warm climate, but fogs are common in the summer months.

You may encounter language problems because of the many nationalities.

Take care! The streets of San Francisco are not paved – let alone paved with gold!

Gold can be discovered as flakes, dust or nuggets. Mining is hard work and few make their fortune.

San Francisco is an exciting place to visit. The harbour is packed with ships, and every day 30 new buildings are built. Theatres, hotels and saloons have sprung up all over the city.

Sightseers' tip

Many of the ships in the harbour have been abandoned by passengers and crew rushing off to the gold diggings.

Getting there

To get to San Francisco by sea you can travel either around South America's Cape Horn, or via Panama. The Cape Horn journey can take seven months and you will have to contend with storms, overcrowding and boredom. The Panama route is quicker, but more expensive. Travellers have to pay extra to cross the narrow neck of land between North and South America.

Sea travellers are often called "argonauts", named after adventurers in Greek mythology who sailed with the hero Jason on his ship *Argo* in search of the Golden Fleece.

San Francisco has no docks so you must wade through mud to reach the shore.

A sea voyage is the only option if travelling in the winter months.

Ships are often so crowded that you may have to sleep in a lifeboat!

Sightseers' tip
Overland travellers will need a very well-equipped wagon. Remember you will be crossing plains, deserts, rivers and mountains, and covering only about 30 kilometres a day.

If you are planning to pan for gold during your stay in San Francisco, a strong mule will help you carry your mining equipment.

Those who choose to journey overland can join other travellers on the banks of the Missouri River. Make sure you pack your wagon with plenty of food, tools and bedding. Although the wagons are uncomfortable (they have no springs), they are sturdy and practical. Most people use oxen to haul their wagons. They are strong, can travel further without water than horses and can be eaten if you run out of food.

What to wear

Practical clothing is a must for visitors to California. Wool shirts and heavy trousers are commonly worn by miners and are ideal for the rough, outdoor life they lead. Make sure you bring a pair of stout boots with you. They will protect your feet from the ankle-deep mud that floods the streets of San Francisco.

For the ultimate gold rush souvenir why not buy a woollen shirt with a shovel and pick motif?

Sightseers' tip

Make sure you wear a wide-brimmed hat to protect you from the sun while panning for gold. Try rubbing bear fat into the leather of your boots to make them waterproof.

Miners tend to have poor hygiene. They do not wash themselves very often.

You will be on your feet all day, so make sure you bring a sturdy pair of shoes.

As with everything else in California, clothes are very expensive.

Thousands of Chinese immigrants have flocked to California in recent years. Many dress in a traditional Chinese style, wearing pointed, broad-brimmed hats and loose-fitting clothes. The men grow their hair long and tie it in a single plait.

Many Chinese immigrants have opened up laundries in the mining camps and towns. For a small price, they will take in your dirty clothes and wash them for you.

Long skirts, vast petticoats and bonnets are standard wear for women and girls. Some women dress in men's clothes so they can work more freely and avoid unwanted attention from men.

Don't worry about getting a haircut as uncut, unwashed and uncombed hair is highly fashionable. Long, unkempt beards and whiskers are also de rigueur. This is just as well – most of the region's barbers have gone prospecting in the gold mines! Although many residents of California do not concern themselves with good hygiene and cleanliness, there are plenty of bathhouses in San Francisco. You can make your own soap by boiling water, wood ash and bear fat together in a big kettle.

9

Food and drink

The wide variety of restaurants in San Francisco offers the discerning traveller the chance to sample many traditional foods from all over the world. American, French, German, Mexican and Chinese cooking styles are all to be found in this cosmopolitan city.

It has become the custom to celebrate a lucky strike in the gold mines with a feast of oysters.

Despite the large selection of foods available, most miners have a very poor diet. Food is expensive, particularly outside San Francisco. Fresh vegetables, fruit and dairy products are very hard to get hold of – agriculture in the region has largely been abandoned as farm workers have flocked to the gold mines.

1 kg of potatoes costs one cent in New York, but costs $2 in California.

Meats available include beef, mutton, grizzly bear, deer and turtle.

Many miners use their gold pans as plates for food when camping.

Food is usually cooked over an open fire in the camps. Meals are a time to relax and socialize.

In the mining camps the range of food available is more limited than in the city. Pork and beans form the staple diet of most miners. The pork is usually salted or pickled to preserve it. Remember to boil any water before you drink it. The river water is not clean and may give you a serious infection such as dysentery.

If you go to a Chinese restaurant during your stay in San Francisco you will have to eat from a bowl with chopsticks.

Sightseers' tip

Chinese eating-houses have the best reputation in California. Look out for flags hanging over the doors with "Enter and depart in peace" written in Chinese characters.

11

Shopping

Although pricey, San Francisco is a great city for shopping. You will be able to buy everything from food, clothes, household goods and mining tools to luxury items that include Chinese shawls and fans. You can even buy exotic pets such as brightly coloured parrots and raccoons.

A daguerreotype (photograph) framed in Californian gold makes a great holiday souvenir!

Make sure you visit Chinatown. The shops are packed with luxury goods such as this beautiful fan.

If you are planning a trip to the gold mines you will need to purchase mining and camping equipment. The storekeeper should be able to advise you on what tools you will need.

Camp stores sometimes offer overnight shelter to new arrivals.

In newer mining camps the store acts as a social centre for miners.

Travelling artists (failed miners) will, for a price, sketch your diggings.

California is a *very* expensive place to shop! Most miners earn about $10 a day, but a dozen eggs can set you back $4 and a single apple can cost as much as $1. San Francisco has attracted many entrepreneurs. One ship's captain brought a shipload of stray cats to the city and sold them as rat-catchers at $10 apiece.

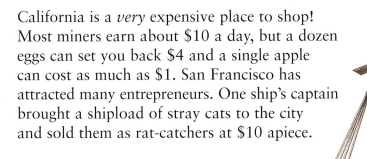

You will find a general store at the centre of most mining camps. As well as supplying miners with essential goods and tools, the store often acts as a bar and gambling den. Every store has a set of scales to weigh the gold dust used by the miners in place of money. Storekeepers will usually offer credit – unless you prove to be a hopeless risk!

Sightseers' tip
Abandoned ships are often run aground and leased as shops and hotels. You may well see some nestling among other buildings in the streets of San Francisco.

Accommodation

Many houses have been prefabricated in the eastern states and shipped around Cape Horn to California.

Y ou will have no problem finding accommodation to suit your budget in San Francisco. If you can't afford to stay in one of the fine hotels in Portsmouth Square, you could opt for a bed in a boarding house or dormitory. If your budget is really tight, why not simply pitch up a tent in one of the mining camps?

While some cabins are very isolated, others are grouped together, forming small towns.

Many miners have built themselves log cabins near their claim. The cabins are usually quite small and cramped. Window glass is very expensive, but some miners have made their own windows by cutting the flat ends from glass jars and gluing several of them into a frame using mud.

Make sure you have a good supply of candles to provide light in your cabin in the evenings.

Prices range from $37 a week for a hotel room, to $6 a week for a dormitory bed.

Many hotels host entertainment and gambling in the evenings.

Watch out for snakes – they get everywhere, including into beds!

HOTEL

San Francisco's grandest hotel is Parker House on Portsmouth Square. The White Cheer House Hotel on Sacramento Street, however, is the only one with bathtubs.

Sightseers' tip

Hotels and boarding-houses in San Francisco don't usually have backyards. You will often see people chatting and children playing on the wooden sidewalks and in the dusty streets in front of their lodgings.

Prospecting for gold

Making your fortune at the gold diggings is not very likely. However, a day spent prospecting would be an interesting excursion, and you never know, you could be lucky! All you need to do is stake your claim on a promising bit of land.

Sightseers' tip

Watch out! Newcomers are usually directed to land in mines such as Poverty Bars, Coyote Diggings, Old Dry Diggings and Rough and Ready, which have already been thoroughly worked over!

Make sure you follow the miners' strict rules for staking a claim.

 Wear comfortable, durable clothes – you will be out in the elements all day.

 Gold dust can be used in shops to pay for food and goods.

Gold is usually found in strips of rock. River water eats away the rock, exposing the gold, and carries it downstream. Look at bends in the river, where the water slows down and deposits the gold.

You can take any gold dust you discover to a local bank. They will weigh it and pay you the going rate – about $1 for 30 grams.

The initial rush of gold fever has used up all the surface gold. So digging for gold is now tedious, back-breaking work. The simplest method of prospecting is panning. This means spending hours squatting in ice-cold water, rotating the pan to separate the gold from the earth. Most miners work in teams, using a cradle or long-tom to speed up the sorting. You can identify gold if you bite it or hammer it – fool's gold will flake.

You will need only simple tools for a day's prospecting – pickaxes to break up the rock, shovels to move the earth and stones, and a pan.

17

Visit a saloon

To get a true taste of Californian life make sure you visit one of the many saloons and gambling dens. In the dimly lit, smoke-filled saloons bar-keepers serve wines and spirits, gossip is exchanged and business transactions take place. The saloons are often elaborately decorated, with ornate fixtures shipped from all over the world. Look out for the spittoons placed on the floor for the benefit of tobacco chewers.

There are few women in mining towns and men often have to take women's roles in dances. The man who dons a hoop petticoat becomes the "belle of the ball"!

Alcohol has many nicknames, including "devil's brew", "rot gut" and "firewater".

Watch out for professional gamblers who usually cheat to make sure they win.

Saloon keepers tend to make more money than gold miners.

Sightseers' tip Miners often pay for drinks with gold dust. When the saloon closes, enterprising children run wet pins between the floorboards to pick up any spilled dust.

The saloons often put on musical entertainment to encourage custom. Female singers are particularly popular.

If you fancy trying your luck at cards you will have no problem finding a game to join. There are over 1,000 gambling dens in San Francisco alone. Popular games include Faro and Twenty-One.

The gambling halls are very profitable for their owners and many offer customers free food and liquor.

19

Leisure time

If you are feeling energetic, why not have a go at the exciting new team game, baseball. Recently introduced from New York, the object of the game is to score more "runs" than the opposing team. Four "bases" are marked in a diamond shape on open ground and the two 9-player teams take turns batting and fielding. A run is made when a batter completes a circuit of all four bases.

Itinerant musicians travel around the mining camps, playing popular songs on banjos.

Look out for the bell ringers employed to draw crowds into the theatres.

There are special mining songs such as "On the Banks of the Sacramento".

Theatre performers often do tours of the mining camps and towns.

Sightseers' tip San Francisco theatres such as the Metropolitan attract full houses most evenings. The cheaper seats are in the pit and the rear balconies.

Baseball games are often played on the Sandlot – a park on the site of San Francisco's old cemetery.

Why not visit one of the many theatres that have sprung up in San Francisco over the last five years. Comedy and singing acts are very popular with audiences, but the latest rage is for child performers. Because of the shortage of women in California, actresses are always well received. Male actors, however, are often booed.

Red-headed Lotta Crabtree is the most famous child star. She sings, dances, recites poems and imitates famous people.

21

Sutter's Mill

Captain John Sutter is a German immigrant. He moved to California in 1839 and acquired a large plot of land from the Mexican governor.

Make sure you visit Sutter's Mill, site of the first gold discovery. In 1847, Captain John Sutter needed lumber for his various building projects, and went into partnership with James Marshall, a carpenter, to build a mill. On 24th January 1848, Marshall was making his daily inspection of the sawmill when he discovered pieces of gold in the water.

Sightseers' tip Another historic building worth a visit is Mission Dolores. Founded by Franciscan monks in 1776, the tile-covered, white-walled church is dedicated to St Francis. Take time to admire the gilded altar, painted ceilings and Spanish manuscripts.

Sutter tried to keep quiet about the gold find on his land, but newspaper man Sam Brannan made sure news of the gold spread far and wide. He was drumming up trade for his new store, which he had amply stocked with picks, shovels and pans!

Sutter's Mill is on the American River, about 65 kilometres above its junction with the Sacramento River.

Sutter is not profiting from the gold rush as much of his land has been taken by miners.

Mission Dolores is a Roman Catholic church founded by Spanish monks.

Look out for paintings by native Americans on the ceilings of Mission Dolores.

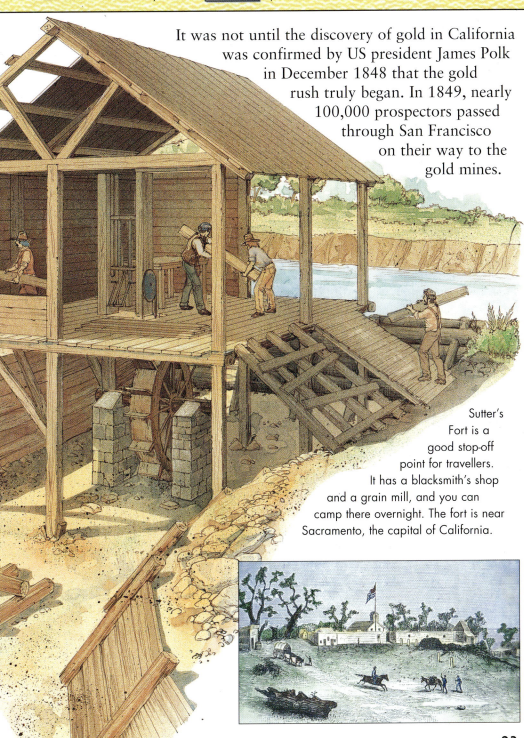

It was not until the discovery of gold in California was confirmed by US president James Polk in December 1848 that the gold rush truly began. In 1849, nearly 100,000 prospectors passed through San Francisco on their way to the gold mines.

Sutter's Fort is a good stop-off point for travellers. It has a blacksmith's shop and a grain mill, and you can camp there overnight. The fort is near Sacramento, the capital of California.

23

The wild west

The state of California is famed for its breathtaking and diverse scenery. In the north, rugged, snow-capped mountain ranges and dense fir, pine and redwood forests dominate the landscape. In contrast, southern California is home to beautiful ocean beaches, the scorching Mojave Desert, and Death Valley, the hottest place in the United States.

Native Americans call Death Valley "Tomesha" – the land where the ground is on fire. This is because it gets so hot that the valley floor shimmers.

California is home to many strange and unique plants. The recently named Joshua trees in southern California can grow as tall as nine metres. Some are believed to be over 1,000 years old.

California is a vast state with few roads. Travel can often be slow and treacherous.

The San Andreas Fault runs through the state, so earthquakes are always possible.

Look out for the many different Native American tribes in California.

Vaqueros (Californio cowboys) keep cattle from wandering off ranch land.

While travelling around California you may well come across a Californio cattle ranch. The Californios are descendants of the original Spanish settlers. Since the beginning of the gold rush, many Californios have abandoned their ranches to seek their fortunes in the mines.

Sightseers' tip

The largest trees in the world are to be found in northern California. The redwoods, called giant sequoias, can grow to heights of 100 metres and live for over 3,000 years. Remember to look out for the wildlife – deers, foxes and black bears all live in this area.

25

Native American tribes

If you need a break from the hustle and bustle of San Francisco, why not visit a Native American village? The 50 different tribes in California are hunter-gatherers and are very peaceful. They may, however, be suspicious of strangers – the gold rush is destroying their traditional way of life.

Sightseers' tip

The Miwok tribe live in round bark houses called "u-ma-cha", and in the centre of the village is a large ceremonial house. The Miwoks wear feather costumes during their ceremonial dances.

Native Americans have few rights. Legally, they can be treated as slaves.

Acorns make up the staple food – they are crushed and made into a gruel.

Native American crafts are widely admired all over the world.

Many Californian tribes are famed for their detailed basketry.

Strings of dentalium shells are highly valued and are often used as money by Native American tribes in California. The longer the shell, the greater the value!

The constant activity in and around rivers by gold miners has polluted the water and killed many of the fish. It has also weakened the oak trees, affecting the acorn harvest on which the Native Americans depend. Many of the tribes have also been wiped out by diseases brought into the area by the miners, or suffered terrible persecution at the hands of the prospectors. It seems unlikely that the Native American traditions will survive much longer.

Native Americans make very comfortable leather shoes called moccasins. Sometimes they will trade these for miners' boots.

Survival guide

Visitors to California should remember that it is a fledgling state. As most goods have to be shipped to San Francisco, prices are very high. There is not much infrastructure – laws are invented off the cuff, transport facilities are limited, and life is very rough and ready.

Law and order

To counter the lack of law enforcement, a group of San Francisco citizens banded together in 1851 and formed a "Vigilance Committee". Criminal offenders are hauled before the Committee and made to account for their actions. Very often the accused are flogged as punishment, but for serious crimes, such as murder, the punishment is hanging. The Committee makes its own rules and is known to punish people without trial.

Punishment is often swift. It is not unheard of for criminals to be caught, tried and hanged on the same day.

Health

Try to avoid falling ill during your visit to California. Doctors will charge 30 grams of gold just for looking at your tongue!

Cholera, diphtheria, dysentery and scurvy are all common diseases. Standing in cold water for long hours while panning for gold has given many miners rheumatism. Native American tribes have been badly affected by diseases carried by miners.

Disease is rife and one in five miners in California dies every year.

It is worth spending money on expensive fruit and vegetables to combat scurvy.

The Democratic Party is in power in most parts of California.

Administration

Fires are very common in San Francisco. The wooden buildings are often close together and fire takes hold very easily. Volunteer fire companies have formed all over the city to combat the frequent infernos. Membership of the fire companies is a great honour and there is much rivalry between the city's different companies.

After every fire, San Francisco is rebuilt swiftly. New buildings are often put up while fires are still smouldering.

Hundreds of men using long ropes haul the hose wagons and fire engines to the scene of the fire.

29

❓ Souvenir quiz

Take your time exploring California. It is a fascinating and varied land with plenty to see and experience. Before you leave, test your knowledge with this fun quiz. You will find the answers on page 32.

1. Why are gold prospectors in California often called "forty-niners"?

a) Because California is the 49th state of the United States.

b) Because 1849 was the year that most prospectors travelled to California.

c) Because the average age of the prospectors is 49.

2. Shopping is expensive because most goods have to be shipped to San Francisco. Why are vegetables and dairy products so expensive?

a) Because agriculture has largely been abandoned as farm workers flock to the gold mines.

b) Because the land in California is very poor.

c) Because there is not much demand for fresh food.

3. Why is it sensible to bring a pair of stout boots with you to California?

a) Because they are considered the height of fashion.

b) To protect your feet from the mud that floods the streets of San Francisco.

c) To stop grizzly bears from picking up your scent.

4. How can you tell gold from fool's gold?

a) Fool's gold flakes when you bite it or hammer it.

b) Real gold is a different colour from fool's gold.

c) Fool's gold has a distinct odour, while real gold is odourless.

5. Miners in California have coined many new words and expressions. What is "firewater"?

a) A unique natural phenomenon in Death Valley where flames rise from a pool of water.

b) A lake near San Francisco from which water is pumped to fight the city's many fires.

c) A nickname used by miners to describe alcohol.

6. The largest trees in the world can be found in California. What are they?

a) Joshua trees.

b) Sequoia redwoods.

c) Oak trees.

7. Baseball is a new team game that is becoming very popular in California. What is a "run"?

a) A circuit of the four bases.

b) The name of the pitch.

c) A bet on the outcome of a game.

8. Gold was discovered at the site of Sutter's Mill in 1848. Who actually made the discovery?

a) Captain John Sutter, owner of the mill.

b) Sam Brannan, a newspaper owner.

c) James Marshall, a carpenter.

9. Native American tribes have had their traditional way of life destroyed by the gold rush. What do many Californian tribes use as money?

a) They don't use money – all goods are bartered (exchanged).

b) Gold and gems.

c) Strings of dentalium shells.

10. What is the usual punishment for murder?

a) Flogging.

b) Life imprisonment.

c) Death by hanging.

Index

Acknowledgements

Kingfisher would like to thank
Noreen Studdart for additional research.

The consultant
Christina Parker, B.A., P.G.C.E. is Education Officer
at the American Museum in Britain, Bath.

Design assistance
Joanne Brown

Inklink Firenze illustrators
Simone Boni, Alessandro Rabatti, Lorenzo Pieri,
Luigi Critone, Lucia Mattioli, Francisco Petracchi,
Theo Caneschi.

Additional illustrations
Peter Dennis, Shirley Tourret.

Picture credits
b = bottom, c = centre, l = left, r = right, t = top
p.5tl Science Museum/ET Archive; p.6tl Peter Newark's
American Pictures; p.10cl The Anthony Blake Photo Library;
p.11cr Christie's Images; p.12tr The Bancroft Library/University of
California, br Fitzwilliam Museum, University of Cambridge/The
Bridgeman Art Library, London; p.14tl from *The Pocket Guide
to California* by J.E. Sherwood, New York 1849, (RB1152)/The
Huntington Library, San Marino, California, br Iris & B. Gerald
Cantor Center for the Visual Arts at Stanford University; Stanford
Family Collections, 12083; p.21br Brown Brothers; p.22tl Peter
Newark's Pictures; p.23br Peter Newark's Pictures; p.24cl
Corbis UK/David Paterson; p.29tr The Oakland Museum
of California, Kahn Collection.

*Every effort has been made to trace the copyright holders
of the photographs. The publishers apologise for any
inconvenience caused.*

Souvenir quiz answers

1 = b)   2 = a)   3 = b)   4 = a)   5 = c)   6 = b)   7 = a)   8 = c)   9 = c)   10 = c)